AF417696

REVEREND BUDDY AARON LARRIER

A MAN OF VISION WITH A MISSION OF HOPE

Foreword by Adolphus Grazette former Chairman of Barbados Overseas Citizens
Association (BOCA)


Published by: Non-State Actors Reparations Commission Inc.



ISBN 978-976-96223-4-0

Paper back: US$15.00 / UK15.00, Ebook: US$5.00 / UK5.00

# CONTENTS


Foreword      5

Message of Hope      7

Early Beginnings      8

The Vision      13

The Mission of Hope      15

Barbados We Gatherin' 2020      42

Bridgetown City of Peace      44

Recommendation      45

Acknowledgements      49

Vision      51

Summary      53

# FOREWORD

The Rev. Aaron Buddy Larrier or Buddy as he is affectionately known is a truly remarkable man. Born into a large family of poor black Barbadians, receiving only basic education, Buddy set out to educate himself. His father died in 1955 during the passage of Hurricane 'Janet' at that time he was only 12 years old. Buddy found that working for a living and gaining an education was an arduous task, so when the call from the Mother Country came to encourage Barbadians to widen their horizons he was ready to accept the challenge.

Buddy immigrated to England in 1963, and it was there that he was awakened to the role he had to play in the struggle that the African Race had been engaged in for centuries. It was in the UK where Buddy began to understand the form of overt racism that most Black people endured. Buddy continued his self-education and after a short break when he lived in the USA he returned to the UK to continue his mission in life. Having armed himself with knowledge he began the real work. I first met Buddy Larrier in 1984, at that time I was the Secretary of a local NGO, called Barbados Overseas Citizens Association (BOCA). 'BOCA' was a Bajan organisation started by me and two other Barbadians, Namely Frank Jackman (deceased) and Michael Smith.

My first encounter with Buddy was somewhat frightening, the concepts and pronunciations the Brother expounded were beyond my limited grasp at the time. After some reflection I decided I needed to know the Brother, to understand what he was about, I therefore set up a meeting at his residence, where we talked for several hours. The following are my findings:-

The Reverend Bro. Aaron Buddy Larrier is a true Visionary. When credit is being given to persons for the initiative of We Gatherin' 2020 Reverend Aaron Buddy Larrier must be among them. He is a soldier in the battle to free the African Race from the cloak of Racism. He has dedicated his life to the struggle for our survival and is ever engaged in the effort to awaken his Brethren. In 1985 Bro. Larrier was part of the Executive Committee of BOCA, during a conversation with me Mike Smith and Frank Jackman (Founder Members of BOCA) Buddy made this prediction. "THE JOBS YOU NOW HOLD WILL SOON BE REQUIRED FOR WHITE PEOPLE". At that time all three of us were Middle Managers in London Transport Bus Garages. I was at Upton Park Bus Garage, and Michael and Frank were at West Ham Bus Garage. Also at that time 50% of the Middle Managers in London Transport Executive Company (Buses & Underground) were Black, mostly West Indians who had answered the call in the early 60s. The same was true for the Post Office. By the year of 1989 they were all out of these organisations. All of the Black Middle Managers had worked their way up through the system that was in place when we entered the UK. The company divested them of their positions by changing the systems. One must now have a college degree to attain these positions.

Brother Aaron Buddy Larrier, a true Visionary with Messages of Hope.

CARIBBEAN TIMES *incorporating African Times* TUESDAY, 23 OCTOBER 1990

## Proposal for Hope 1990 Relevant for today

The Barbados High Commission in London was the setting in 1990 for what should have been one of the most significant contributions towards world peace in the 1990s. It was the place where the proposal for a "Universal Day of Hope" was launched.

The author of this proposal, Buddy Larrier, is a social historian who was born in Barbados and lived in England for over 30 years.

The proposal is directed primarily to non-European nations calling on them individually or collectively through the United Nations to declare October 12 a **Universal Day of Hope** and for it to start from October 1992. It also appeals to European nations to do likewise.

October 12, 1992 was significance because it marked the 500th anniversary of Columbus' arrival in the "New World".

The proposal gives a historical analysis of the way politics, economics, religion and race/racism have affected the lives of all the world's people as a direct result of that initial adventure by Christopher Columbus in 1492.

Present at the launch were representatives from other High Commissions, industry, educational establishments, churches, the private and voluntary sectors along with friends, relatives and other acquaintances. The proceedings were opened with a prayer from Rev. Dr. Sehon Goodridge, a fellow Barbadian.

The launch was chaired by the Deputy High Commissioner Owen Eversley.OBE.

He went on to ask those in attendance to use their positions and influence as he intended, to ensure that their governments do all within their power to assist and make the proposal a reality.

### Speaker

Guyanese-born Mrs. Sybil Phoenix MBE, was the guest speaker, she said that it was in December last year that Mr. Larrier first informed her that he was inspired to make a proposal to the world.

"I was very much taken back by the magnitude of his vision," she said.

As for the inspiration that led him to formulate the proposal, Larrier said "I had a vision back in 1977 and as a result, my whole life has been transformed. It has changed to such a degree that at times it is difficult to believe that I am the same person as before."

The Rt. Rev. Dr. Sir. Wilfred Wood, former Bishop of Croydon, said of Mr. Larrier, "The theme of his call is unity... the unity of the people of Barbados and the people of the world."

Buddy Larrier with his Peace Proposal to the people of the world - 1990

Years after the launch of his proposal this visionary elder, Reverend Buddy A. Larrier, founder and president of the **'Universal Day of Hope Trust'** is still in pursuit of his mission.

In 1995, he submitted a resolution for October 12, to be a Day of Hope for truth, justice and peace to the Government of Barbados for consideration.

In 2001, he presented the resolution to the 168 nation states gathered at the historic United Nations World Conference Against Racism, which was held in Durban, South Africa and in 2002, the resolution was endorsed at the Afrikan and Afrikan Descendants World Conference against Racism, which was held in Barbados. In April 2008 the resolution was also endorsed by the 16th District of the African Methodist Episcopal (AME) Church Windward Islands.

# EARLY BEGINNINGS

The birth of any child is a miracle. This I found out in 1987. The miracle of my birth in the beautiful Caribbean Island of Barbados occurred on July 2, 1943 and I was Christened Buddy Aaron Larrier. This was during the time when World War II also known as the Second World War was at its peak. World war 11 like World War 1 was a European family affair that affected the global community and lasted from 1939 to 1945. The vast majority of the world's countries including all the great powers were involved, and its impact on small colonized developing countries was severe. Barbados being a colony of Britain persons born in Barbados were British subjects and as a result a number of them enlisted to fight in the war in support of their "Mother Country" as England was so considered. Even the father of our independence His Excellency and National Hero Errol Walton Barrow was a pilot in the British Army. My birth might have been influenced by the revolutionary spirit of that time.

As a youth I grew up in the fishing community of Oistins Town in the parish of Christ Church, and was the seventh of 11 children of Minnie Glendora Lashley-Larrier and Darnell Dacosta Larrier. I was the first of the siblings that was privilege to take what is now known as the common entry (11 plus) exam in 1954. Our family was from the lower peasantry working class of the community. Our father was born in the United States of America (USA), both his father and mother Aaron and Essie Larrier was born in St. Philip but immigrated during the early 1900s when the Panama Canal was being built and settled in New York, USA . They had two children and sent our dad and his sister Lilian back to Barbados for their early education. The Larriers was and is an established family name in St. Philip, it is said that all Larriers are related and that we originated from St. Philip. As a youth our dad had options, after his early schooling his mother wanted him to return to the USA with his sister, but he had other plans, he could have chosen a profession which his family wanted him to pursue, but he had a passion for the Sea as if driven by destiny of a compelling spirit. To avoid the pressure from the family in St. Philip he moved to Oistins and became a fisherman. The family was very disappointed at his choice because Fisherfolk were considered the lowest of persons, and being a fisherman was one of the most dangerous professions at the time. Our mother was from the parish of Christ Church, she was a domestic servant and a community midwife, an admirable and respected profession she inherited from her mother Matilda Linton.

All our siblings started education at the Christ Church Boys and Girls Primary Schools. I left school at age 15 years old because I did not gain a place at a secondary school. I was the first of the siblings that was privilege to take the common entry (11 plus) exam in 1954, but was not given a pass. Our mum was very disappointed; she had expected me to gain a place to attend the Christ Church Foundation School. However, it was not long before she understood the reasons why I was denied entrance to a secondary school in Barbados. One year later on September 22, 1955 Barbados experienced its worst natural disaster since 1895 when Hurricane Janet a category four hurricane struck the island causing much destruction and claiming the lives of some 38 persons. The parish of Christ Church was greatly affected in particular the fishing community of Oistins. Our father was one of two fishermen that went missing at sea during the passage of the hurricane. Hurricane Janet turned out to be a blessing in disguise for our family. Neither of the two bodies of the fishermen was recovered and due to the devastation caused by the hurricane the government set up a Social Fund to assist those families that were most affected. Our father left mum with nine of his children, six of whom were under 16 years old. We benefited greatly.  Pearline an elder sister who was age 18 at the time was given a free passage to England and four brothers and two sisters under the age of 16 were later assisted with a trade after leaving primary school or given a lump sum on reaching age 21. None of the boys chose fishing as a career, I decided on tailoring to help the family. Throughout my youth I was known for my daring and courageous spirit, and was seen as a leader among my peers, I was also a body builder at the Sea Breeze Club near Oistins and was popular with the girls. During the 1960s there were push and pull factors surrounding immigration to England. The slogan "Your Mother Country Need You" along with the rumour that the streets of England were paved with gold was the pull factor. The high level of unemployment in Barbados and the Caribbean was the push factor. By 1963 I was a self employed tailor but we were all caught up in the euphoria of the pull and push factors, many of my peers from school days were immigrating. I had the opportunity of choice either the USA or England, I decided like many thousands of British born Caribbean nationals to be part of the adventure to the "Mother Country"; my decision was influenced also because six of my siblings were already there. I was recruited to work with London Transport Board as a Bus Conductor, which apart from the nursing profession was the best available job open to immigrants from the British colonies. During this period Barbados was classified as "Little England" and was the only colony whereby persons were given assurance of a job before leaving their country of birth. However, my experience in England was that of an unwanted child.

Like most persons that were immigrating to England I too was expected to spend only five years because of the rumour throughout the Caribbean that "the streets of England were paved with gold" and we would have been back home with lots of money. Where the rumour came from was not of interest, the fact is, it was believed by most young people. It was so attractive that I gave up a lucrative professional tailoring business for a bus conducting job in a cold and hostile environment. Most persons like me on arriving in England would have returned home if we had the airfare, but we were on contract.

My mother and I had a very close relationship and as my first child (a son) was born in September 1963 just two months before I immigrated I asked her to look out for him and promised her that if I did not return home in five years I would send for her on holiday. Within one year of arriving in England it was clear that the five years plan of returning home was not going to be realised because there was no gold on the streets of London, but much cold. In 1964 I sent for the mother of my son Andrew and in 1967 sent for mum to spend her 56th birthday with my siblings, which placed her among the very few mothers who would have went on holiday to England during the 1960s when Barbadians were immigrating in great numbers. In hindsight it is evident that this was another of God's plan for the family and for me personally. By 1967 when mum arrived in England I was the father of two other children both girls. Mum being a midwife and care giver back in her Christ Church community was very concern about the arrangement for the social wellbeing of her grandchildren in England. Being conscious of the culture in Barbados whereby families looked after each other's children she insisted that on her return to Barbados she would be taking the children with her. During this time there were other siblings in England who also had children but the children that mum were most concern about was mine. The social care that mum was concerned about in England was part of the unconscious racism that was obscured from us black people who were seeking social care for our children when working. All immigrants were looking for employment and there were no options but to leave our black children in the care of white women, whereby you drop them off at the front door on your way to work and pick them up at the front door on your way home. Mum felt this was not the environment she wanted her grandchildren to experience.

It was not until years later in 1977 when my eyes were opened that I fully understood the type of racism that mum saw in 1967. The reality was that all black immigrants who went to England from the 1950s and 1960s experienced overt racism but most of us endured it because of survival, and working on either the buses or trains was one of the better jobs for black people in England. By the 1970s I felt that the time had come for me to escape from the clutches of racism and to return home even without the expected riches. Therefore, in 1972 I gave up my secured job on the buses and returned to Barbados with the intention of resettling for good, but our eldest sister Pauline persuaded me to join her in New York, she had lived in England and also worked as a bus conductor but had moved to New York, and was in Barbados on holiday. I gave in to her wishes and in December of 1972 I went to New York. To my astonishment within the first week in the city that never sleeps I was held at gun point when two persons robed the facility of the workplace where I was visiting a friend. That experience convinced me that the United States of America was not the place I wanted to live. With that as a motivating factor in 1974 I returned to England via Barbados.

However, it was in New York that my eldest sister informed me of the significance of my birth, which according to her was due to a revelation of our grandmother. I worked with the London Transport Board until 1977 when I had an epiphany – a vision with a mission similar as in the book of Jeremiah 1: 5-8; *"before I formed thee in the belly I knew thee; and before thou camest forth out of the womb I sanctified thee, and I ordained thee a prophet unto the nations….. be not afraid of their faces; for I am with thee to deliver thee saith the Lord."*

This booklet is an introduction to my life's work as part of the instructions given to me by God the Creator and or the ancestors for the Government of Barbados to take certain action that would guide the world out of its present state of confusion. This was confirmed on February 27, 2020 by Professor Sir Hilary Beckles, Vice Chancellor of the University of the West Indies (UWI) who gave a lecture as one of We Gatherin' events for the parish of St. Peter with the theme 'From Cuffee to Owen'. That presentation by Sir Hilary who is one of the World's most recognised and outstanding historians, scholars and intellectuals can be considered as the icing on the cake for what is recommended to the Government and people in this Booklet as action to be taken.

# THE VISION

I consider myself a man of vision with a mission of hope from an African centred perspective, as it is evident that either God the Creator or the ancestors had a special assignment for me with the preparation for my entrance into the world on Friday, July 2, 1943 – the same date and day of the week as my grandmother who was also born on Friday, July 2, 1875 and of my mother who was born on Sunday, July 2, 1911. The odds of such unusual births are considered as high as 1 in 40 million; and even higher if we take into consideration that a family in New Mexico of grandmother, mother and child share the same July 2, birth date (1962, 1985 and 2014). According to our eldest sister our grandmother had a premonition about my birth. By 1941 our mother had six children but was not married and our grandmother confronted her with an ultimatum that she and my dad had to get married before I was conceived or else, which they did. I became the first Larrier of mum and dad, and her seventh child of eleven children sharing the unique birthdates grandmother, mother and child. Therefore, the relationship between my mother and I was precious to me. Mum was very pleased about my decision not to stay in New York and to return to Barbados before going back to England. On my return to England in 1974 I rejoined the London Transport Board as a Bus Driver. Three years later in 1977 I had a minor operation on the little finger of my right hand, which was later considered to have been experimental and was also unsuccessful. While recovering from the surgery I had an epiphany; **the vision of "a vivid picture of a New Political and Economic Order for the 21st century based on truth, justice and peace; new political awakening for Barbadian and other people of the Caribbean region, as leaders in world affairs; the uniting of my family as a single unit towards family unity of African people; the acquisition of economic power by 'black people and the end of Apartheid in South Africa and of global oppression of 'White Supremacy' (Racism)".** Trying to come to terms with the vivid picture in my mind of what was to happen in 30 years was a challenge, and no one around me understood what I was going through. Subsequently, I was sectioned under the 1959 Mental Health Act and detained in a mental institution. My compulsory detention was under section 25 of the 1959 act for 28 days which could have been extended to section 26 for up to a year. My vision and mission were considered a form of madness (if it is I hope they never find a cure). I was given drugs against my will that was having adverse effects on my mental state. Within one week of being sectioned mum travelled from Barbados to England to be at my side, because she was convinced in her spirit that I could not have been mentally ill. It was then that I informed her of the vision and the mission that was given to me, and she immediately understood that my detention was part of the preparation for my mission. With that assurance from her three weeks later I came to term with the power that dwells within. I challenged the consultant and demanded my release that same day. As a result I became the first known person (black or white) to have done such in British history. The Independent Television (ITV) network of England was so impressed with news of my victory of gaining release from Bexley Mental Institution that they made two documentaries entitled 'Patients or Prisoners' (1979) and 'Skin: Racism and Mental Health' (1981) exposing the abuse of power under the mental health act. They used my experience as the main focal, which is evident in the documentaries Youtube link below.

https://www.youtube.com/watch?v=lb-QMLJD5vQ&feature=em-upload_
owner

# THE MISSION OF HOPE

*Bishop Dr. Sir Wilfred Wood*
*Former Bishop of Croydon England*

*This is a story, simply told, of one man's struggle, in adversity, to pursue a vision which came out of his knowledge of himself as someone of worth – a child of God. Neither the misreading of his action, the misdiagnosis of his condition or the lack of comprehension of his religious convictions on the part of others was able to deter him from following what he believed was a call from God. The theme of the call was unity, just as there is a unity of the circle made when a stone is dropped into a pool, so there is an underlying bond in the unity of the Larrier family, the unity of the people of Barbados and the Unity of the people of the world. Buddy Larrier's mission is a reminder that "it is always better to light a candle than merely curse the darkness". Each person big or small, can do as Buddy did and begin where he or she is, I hope others will be inspired by his story to follow his example".*

*The above was taken from the book Pride and Unity: Dawn of a New Era Barbados and the Larrier family (1989).*

My first assignment of the vision was to undertake the mission of uniting my family as a single unity after years of separation following Hurricane Janet of 1955. The first attempt of re-uniting the family was on July 2, 1978 to celebrate our mother's 67th birthday. That event was the first International Family Reunion for Barbadians. It was also to thank the people and Government of Barbados for the assistance given to the family following Hurricane Janet, but it was not fully successful as two brothers were not in attendance. The second reunion took place eight years later on July 2, 1986 and was a success as all her children and grandchildren were present along with other relatives from the Diaspora. At this gathering the decision was made that the family should establish a business that would cater to the economic secure of future generations of the Larrier Family Clan. Larrier Enterprises Limited an Import and Export business was established. Two years later in 1988 there was a wider extended family reunion that was coordinated by the Larriers from the United States of America. The next reunion was in 2012, which was followed coincidentally by a reunion that was scheduled for July 3-5, 2020 as a joint venture between the Austin and Larrier family in Panama.

My efforts to honour our mother was due mainly because of the close relationship we had. However, in the process of honouring her I was taught a great lesson. One year after our second reunion I became aware that there was a greater lesson to be learned for

*Minnie Larrier with her ten children at the reunion on July 2, 1986*

honouring her, it was on September 6, 1987 when I had the privilege to be present at the birth of the last of my seven children Sayeedah Larrier-Supersad. This is when I became consciously aware of the value of woman that in bringing fourth life the woman risks her own life. Therefore, we should all honour our mothers and woman generally. Since that experience I have had a different perspective of the biblical story of Adam and Eve.

*Some of her children, grandchildren, great grands and other relatives*

*Nieces honouring the future Matriarch on her 80th birthday*

# The Foundation Of Family Unity Is The Woman

Pearline the pioneer who led the family venture to England in 1955 made her first visit to Africa – Uganda - in 2017 to attend a wedding, not consciously knowing it was also in search of her African roots, while there she celebrated her 81st birthday with her African family.

To honour this Elder for reaching out to her African family at age 81 she was crowned Matriarch of our family on July 2, 2018, age 82 years old. On that date the State of African Diaspora was established to unite the 350 million Diasporians with their families on the continent.

# Barbadian seeking relatives worldwide

Mr. Buddy Larrier, a Barbadian living in England, is continuing the campaign to trace all of his relatives who are scattered around the world.

He started this campaign in 1978 when he and his nine brothers and sisters from England, New York and Canada met in Barbados to celebrate their mother's 67th birthday on July 2.

This year the Larriers are planning another reunion but according to Buddy it will be one with a difference for he wants all Larriers to be present.

"We want to set up close family ties so that everyone can have automatic family support when they need it," he said in a recent interview in The Voice, a London newspaper.

Buddy's son, Andrew Larrier, told the Barbados Advocate recently that during this special reunion, they would set up long-term goals for the Larrier family and would draw up an agenda for future plans.

So far, Buddy has traced his 11 brothers and sisters, all of their

Mr. Buddy Larrier, a Barbadian who is in search of his roots, has been living in England for the past 23 years. He is a community worker in Lewisham.

children and two distant cousins, who were adopted after their mother died. Among those relatives he has located are 14 from London, 11 from the United States and two from Canada.

While Buddy is continuing his search in England, his son Andrew is doing his part here at home, for both believe that "African people all over the world must begin to take action which will determine their own destiny" and that one good way to do this is through the family unit."

This year's family reunion is scheduled for August, so Andrew is asking all Larriers in Barbados to contact him at 428-8273.

Buddy Larrier will be going to Sierra Leone later this year to begin his search there for "the original Larriers."

Buddy's mother is Mrs. Larrier of Oistins Hill, Christ Church. His sisters and brothers are: Lionel Lashley and Winfield Lashley from England; Mrs. Pearline Saunders, Mrs. Goldie Davis and Mrs. Beryl Sayers from Canada; Eukline Larrier from the United States; Mrs. Pauline Callender, Perry Larrier, Selwyn Larrier who are living here and the late Darnell Larrier.

Their father the late Darnell "Sonny" Larrier, a fisherman, was among those Barbadians who died during Hurricane Janet in 1957.

Barbados, June 1986

My first book was published in 1989 and entitled 'Pride and Unity; The Dawn of a New Era, Barbados and the Larrier family Unit', this Youtube documentary link below complemented the book.

https://www.youtube.com/watch?v=H7lsBPb-ElY&feature=em-upload_owner

The second assignment in the mission was to challenge the mental health act. In 1978 I started Litigation against the British Health Authority for the violations of my human rights. News of my courageous activism spread and I was invited to be the Chairman of the local Mental Health Association in the London Borough of Lewisham and also to be a member of the National Association for Mental Health (MIND) Executive Board. It was then that I learnt and better understood why throughout the Caribbean it was said that all people returning from England were Mad. In 1987 I represented MIND at the World Conference on Mental Health held in Cairo, Egypt at which I presented a paper on the question; 'What Role Does Racism Play in Psychiatry'?

THE LAUNCH OF THE BETTER LIFE CAMPAIGN 1987: A delegation from the National Association for Mental Health (MIND) to No 10 Downing Street. The delegation which included the Rt Hon Lord Ennals chairperson of the council of management, Chris Heginbotham National Director, Ruth Evans assistant Director and Buddy Larrier Council of Management.

# Race and mental health on Cairo conference agenda

By Michael Mattus

A MAN who has consistently challenged the political implications arising from the (mis)diagnosis of black people as mentally ill has taken his argument to the World Conference on Mental Health being held in Cairo this week.

Buddy Larrier arrived in Egypt last week as part of the British delegation participating in the five-day conference that commenced on Sunday (October 18).

A recently published report, based on six years of research, shows that black people born in Britain are twelve times more likely to be diagnosed and treated as schizophrenic than young white people.

This and the impending enforcement of the Nationality Act lead Mr Larrier to conjecture that a conference of this nature should — as happened the last time it was held in London two years ago — include racism on its agenda.

Mr Larrier's interest stems from an incident in 1977 where he found himself wrongfully arrested and committed to a mental hospital. The details of his arrest and incarceration are very similar to those that ended in the tragic death in custody of Richard "Cartoon".

Compiled in 1980

Since overcoming the difficulties engendered by drug therapy Mr Larrier has established the Afro-Caribbean Mental Health Association and presently chairs the Lewisham chapter of MIND, the mental health charity.

## ACTION

MIND, which has recently launched a Better Life campaign revolving around community care and the after effect of closing large mental institutions, has also been concerned with the effect that racism has on the mental well-being of young black persons born

given non citizens resident in Britain until December 31 1987 to register and the fears for the repercussions that will follow the implementation of these pieces of legislation.

"The police or any other authority would be empowered to certify someone as mentally unstable on the flimsiest of evidence and this would allow deportation orders to be served on a person under sections 86 and 144 of the Mental Health Act, or stay in the country," said Mr Larrier.

See Comment page 8

*Caribbean Times*, London 23rd October 1987

In 1988 I was awarded for my activism in community work. My priority mission was and is African family unity as was given to me in the vision of 1977 as a mission that must be completed in the 21st century. This third decade of the century has started with much hope that the long journey towards the unity of African people is now imminent.

Caribbean Times Friday 3rd to Thursday 9th June 1988

# B.A. Larrier

Buddy A Larrier was born in Barbados and came to England in 1963. He first worked as a bus conductor and later as a driver, staying with London Transport until 1977. Buddy then returned to studies, attending the South West College where he followed courses in Accounts and Book-keeping.

In 1980, he became involved in voluntary community work in the Borough of Lewisham, later becoming an Administrator. Buddy Larrier then specialised in Management Training for black people, working as a Co-ordinator and Development Worker. At present, he is the Co-ordinator and Training Officer specialising in Anti-racist training, "TALIBAH".

Buddy Larrier's main interest is Mental Health, and he was one of the founder members of the Afro-Caribbean Health Association in Lambeth. He is involved in the National Association for Mental Health (MIND) on both a regional and a national level. He also presented a paper at the World Conference on Mental Health in Cairo, Egypt, in 1987.

Buddy Larrier's other interests include promoting greater understanding between cultural groups and to this end he is involved in organising educational International Exchange Programmes.

The island of Barbados is small in size but very big is stature with a peculiar but interesting history. It is said that wherever black people are found in the Western World you will find Barbadians and that one of them would have made an outstanding contribution to their host country. The Prime Minister of Saint Vincent and the Grenadines the Hon. Dr. Ralph Everard Gonsalves has concluded that "Barbados is more than a country - that it is an idea". Barbadians are among the most effected of Diaspora Africans in terms of lost identity. Therefore, it is believe by some that when Barbadians realise who they really are the rest of the African people will come to terms with their identity.

# Blacks urged to find a sense of identity

Black Barbadians have been called upon to find a sense of identity as blacks.

This call came from Mr. Buddy Larrier, a Barbadian-born Englishman and Assistant Director of the Marshal Phoenix Parents Association (MPPA) exchange programme in London.

Mr. Larrier, who recently arrived here from Guyana, where an exchange programme is in progress, will lecture the St. John Cultural Youth Group on Sunday about 'Community Spirit'.

The exchange programme which began in 1981 gives students a chance to visit countries and experience their culture. These young people are selected from among the children of the members of the Parents Association. However, other youths are chosen through the local churches and schools. In 1984 a group of Barbadian youths visited London on the exchange programme.

### Ready for unity

While here the Assistant Director will try to convince the youths of their black identity and to show them that the Caribbean is ready for unity.

"We Barbadians are brought up with the mentality that we must leave our homeland for one of the developed countries. This is not so, for once you enter that foreign land you lose the respect you had at home," he warned. "Once you leave you spend the rest of the time trying to return," Mr. Larrier, who spent 23 years trying to return, said.

**MR. BUDDY LARRIER**

According to him the Barbadian culture with all the Crop-Over festivities seemed vibrant but in fact it was under attack.

Barbadians must learn to respect themselves for when we respect ourselves it is then that we command respect of other racial groups, was his view. Bajans are apt to say "I am proud to be a Barbadian but as soon as they utter these words it only means they are ashamed of being something else, mainly an African," Mr. Larrier said.

He added that the Church did not show the people Jesus Christ in his true likeness of an African which he was. If researched this fact and many others would become clear to all, he advised.

Speaking about Guyana Mr. Larrier said, "I was quite impressed by the togetherness of the people, especially the youth. All the propaganda I heard was dispelled when I saw how they have worked towards a sense of purpose, loyalty and identity, this is a sign of unity."

### Dignity questioned

Observing the large number of youths on Kadooment Day, the MPPA Assistant Director questioned their destiny; but after visiting Guyana, it became very apparent that the Guyanese catered to their youths.

He said that if the Caribbean and black people are to become aware of their identity they must read up on their history. If they did this they would see that they are not inferior people.

After next year, Mr. Larrier said, he would no longer be involved in the programme, adding that he had served his purpose.

After five years, Mr. Larrier said, his aspiration for the programme had succeeded. Inter-relationship with youths has begun and now schools have begun inter-school exchange.

As of next year he will set up a business community while in London on his last exchange.

The outgoing officer of MPPA said he was excited at leaving because he knew the youths would continue his work.

*Advocate*, Barbados, 22nd August 1986

To advance the mission I was inspired to specialize in Racism Awareness Training and Black Consciousness Raising and has carried out lectures, seminars and workshops for diverse groups of persons, different agencies and for some of the London Boroughs. Many institutions have benefitted from my training and have proven the effects of my skills and have testified to the fact of my dedication to truth, justice, world peace, healing and reconciliation. This dedication was strengthened during my visit to Egypt Africa in 1987 to attend the World of Mental Health Conference where I placed black people, mental health and racism on the agenda. I was convinced that the time was right for that action.

## England's best known organisation in Racism Awareness

The trip to Cairo Egypt in 1987 was my first visit to Africa. On return to England from Egypt I began to pay more attention to the history of African people, and in December 1989 I attended an International All Faiths conference on global population projection for the decade 1990 to 2000. I represented the Methodist Church as a director of training. During the workshops a presentation was made that the

# Wesley College

Henbury Road, Westbury-on-Trym, Bristol BS10 7QD.
Telephone: 0272-501700

Principal: The Reverend Dr. W. David Stacey

18th June, 1987.

Rev. Donald Eadie,
15 Northover Road,
Westbury-on-Trym,
Bristol, BS9 3LN.
Tel. 0272 509908.


Mr. Dick Meakins,
Methodist Leadership Race Awareness
  Workshops,
54 Camberwell Road,
London, SE5 0EN.


Dear Dick,

I write to set on record our very great appreciation for the work done,
particularly by Buddy Larrier and Joyce this week.  Sybil, as you know, left
us on Monday morning.

This was a large group and could potentially have been a difficult one to
handle.  I want to say that Buddy in particular was absolutely superb.  He
handled us with skill, sensitivity, conviction, humour and grace.  For some
of us these two days included deep healing and liberation.

Patently this man is doing this work out of a very deep sense of Christian
vocation, no man would want to work with our rubbish unless he was committed
to the redemption process!  For some of us he has become a sign of the work
of Christ.

I will be sending on soon the reports from the Workshop.

I have written to Sybil saying that I will of course be leaving here in a
few weeks time.  When you want to set things up in future I suggest you
contact either my successor, Bill Horton, or David Waterman.  Both David and
Neil Richardson have been to the Workshop and are absolutely convinced of
their significance.

With thanks for all you have made possible for us.

Peace,

Donald

world population should not be allowed to increase by the estimated
two billion projected. This to me was a plot to commit genocide of
two billion people over the period, which was very disturbing to me.

Caribbean Community Secretar
Bank of Guyana Building
P.O. Box 10827
Georgetown
Guyana

**Your Ref:**

**Our Ref:**

2 August 1991

Dear Ms. Phoenix,

The Secretary-General has asked me to acknowledge receipt of your letter dated 7 May, 1991 informing about your proposal for a Universal Day of Hope and for the establishment of a Universal Day of Hope Trust and a Steering Committee. The proposal is indeed one that attracts the interest and support of all those who are striving to bring justice, peace and stability to our world.

Unfortunately, the late arrival of your correspondence did not allow sufficient time to consider bringing the matter to the attention of the Conference of Heads of Government of the Caribbean Community at its recently concluded Twelfth Meeting in St. Kitts and Nevis (July 2-4, 1991), as well as to respond to your indication of the willingness of the President of the Steering Committee, Mr. Buddy Larrier, to make himself available to address the Conference on the issue at that meeting. I anticipate, however, that all CARICOM Governments will be aware of the proposal by now since you had indicated in your letter that it has been brought to the attention of all Commonwealth Heads of State (which include those of all CARICOM Member States) and that these Heads of State have been informed of your request to the Government of Barbados to submit to the United Nations, on behalf of Caribbean Countries, a draft resolution on the matter. As such, I am confident that CARICOM Member States will consider and reflect on your proposal with a view to their lending appropriate support.

Please accept my best wishes for every success in your laudable endeavours.

Yours sincerely,

FRANK ABDULAH
DEPUTY SECRETARY-GENERAL

Ms Sybil Phoenix MBE MS
Chairperson
Universal Day of Hope Trust
P.O. Box 180
London SE26 6NJ
ENGLAND

---

Telephone: 02-69281-9 Cable Address: CARIBSEC GUYANA Telex: 2263 CARISEC GY

As I pondered about the seriousness of the genocide plot, I was inspired in January 1990 to write an open letter to world leaders including CARICOM entitled 'A Proposal for A Universal Day of Hope'. After receiving many positive responses, I made my views public through a booklet to the people of the world. The booklet was part of a project and programme of action.

# 'When there are visions there is Hope'

First Edition,
January 1990

Second Edition,
June 1990

The project was launched in 1991 at the Barbados High Commission in London and then at London Borough of Lewisham Town Hall. The special guest for the occasion was no other than my mother who at 80 years old travelled from Barbados to be at my side. In 1992 I also established the 'Society for the Resettlement of Caribbean Nationals' to help in offering nationals a dignified resettlement to the Caribbean.

The other great mentor and mother figure in my life is Dame Reverend Sybil Phoenix MBE who was born in Guyana. She is a Methodist Minister and she taught me most of what I know about community affairs, race relations and Caribbean intergration.

● THE PHOENIX RISES: Sybil proudly displays her plaque

# Proposal for Day of Hope

President of the Universal Day of Hope Trust, Buddy Larrier (right) presents a draft proposal for the observance of the Universal Day of Hope to Permanent Secretary in the Ministry of Foreign Affairs, Peter Laurie (left), while Glenroy Straughn looks on.

THE Universal Day of Hope Trust presented a draft resolution for the Universal Day of Hope, proposed for October 12, to the Ministry of Foreign Affairs.

President of the organisation which was set up specifically to observe this day, **Buddy Larrier**, and delegates met with permanent secretary in the Ministry, **Dr. Peter Laurie** at the Ministry's offices on Friday.

The president explained that for the past five years he had been burdened with a sense of responsibility for Barbados to accept this proposal.

Larrier said the proposal was conceived in January 1990, and communicated to world leaders and National General Organisations (NGOs), asking their support for observation of the day.

He noted that the Hope Trust received "positive and encouraging" responses from Britain, Canada and Australia.

The draft proposal cites **Christopher Columbus'** discovery of the Americas on October 12, 1492, after which Europeans had sought new ways to expand their resources and satisfy their own desires through the exploitation of indigenous populations.

The resolution in part, goes on to say, "And whereas exploitation through expansionism has led to wars, conflict and human suffering of an unacceptably high level since 12 October 1492;

"And whereas since 12 October 1492, the hope of prosperity has evolved from the idea of one race overcoming another (leading to social injustices such as exploitation and slavery) to the establishment of nations which have become interdependent on one another;..."

The delegation on hand for the presentation included Larrier; **Glenroy Straughn**, representing Citizens Against Narcotics (CAN); **William Bradshaw**, the Universal Day of Hope Trust; **Winston Callender**, Association of Independent Candiates; **Roosevelt King**, Commonwealth Liaison Unit of Barbados; Senator **Viola Davis**, Pan African Movement (Barbados); **NIkeal Tafari**, Third Eye Communications; **Dawnay St. John**, Destiny Incorporated; **Kathy Harris**; and **Amha Selassie Coppin** of the Ethiopian Orthodox Church.

The Universal Day of Hope Trust, hopes to promote and educate through sporting, cultural, social and economic activities for a Universal Day of Hope, which assists in bringing about peace and helping to save the environment from further damage.

In accepting the proposal, Laurie said he would undertake to convey the resolution to the Minister.

In 1994 racism attack me again as the system made another attempt to hinder my mission by unjustly sentencing me to nine (9) months imprisonment in the top security prison Belmarsh. My crime was accepting a third-party cheque as investment in my programme for World Peace. As like the mental institution that incarceration was also to prepare me for greater work within my mission. It was in prison that I learnt of the drug culture and the power of money. That prison experience prepared me for my resettlement in Barbados, as a matter of fact, it was an inmate serving a life sentence that advised me to return to Barbados if I got out of prison alive. The inmates were instrumental in helping me to compile a booklet entitle 'The Beast the Devil's Friend'. I returned home in 1994 immediately on being released from prison and I stood as an independent candidate in the general election of that year. In 1995 through the Ministry of Foreign Affairs the proposal for October 12 was presented as a draft resolution for government's consideration.

In 1998 the government established a Commission for Pan-African Affairs - the first of its kind. I was instrumental in its formation but was given the position of a Messenger while carrying out the duties of a Project Officer. In 2001 the same draft resolution for October 12 was among the resolutions presented to the United Nations World Conference against Racism, Racial Discrimination, Xenophobia and Related Intolerance held in Durban, South Africa. Due to my contribution to that historic conference my job title was changed to that of Project Officer, but my claim for retroactive payment of three years being paid as a messenger, which will be my reparations from government is yet to be honoured.

Thinking outside the box is always a challenge. During this time the proposal put forward for truth, justice, peace, healing and reconciliation was considered controversial to those in authority.

## Economic and spiritual liberation in the 21st century

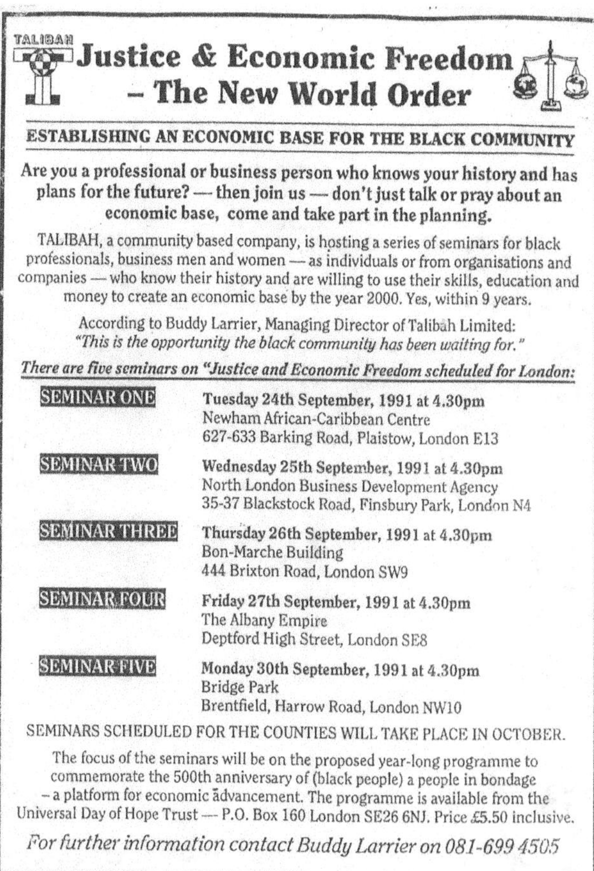

However, it was revolutionary and was supported by Barbadians and other Caribbean national living in England as it included an economic programme.

In 1997 I completed the book 'The Beast the Devil's Friend' that was started in Belmarsh Prison in 1994 and dedicated it to the inmates. My experience in Belmarsh convinced me that violence and crime was a psychological health problem. When the book was produced I made it available to most Barbadian parliamentarians free of charge because it speaks to the issues of the drug culture, violence and crime, dysfunctional families, the unjust capitalist system of white supremacy (Racism) and the need for reparations. It captured the attention of some of the more enlightened persons including some politicians who were concern about the system, which is illustrated in the diagram below and who wanted to bring about change. 'The Beast the Devil's Friend' is now being revised to be launched later this year 2021 or in earlier 2022

## Get to know the Beast and you will understand the system

'The Beast the Devil's Friend' will capture your attention and you will be compelled to share the contents with others. Therefore, if you are a person that lends out your books it is advisable to get two copies, because the chances are that once you lend this booklet out you will not get it back as was the case with some parliamentarians.

*Hon. Mia Amor Mottley, M.P.*
MINISTER OF EDUCATION, YOUTH AFFAIRS AND CULTURE

The Elsie Payne Complex,
Constitution Road,
St. Michael.
Barbados, W.I.

December 15, 1997

Mr. Buddy Larrier
Oistins Hill
**CHRIST CHURCH**

Dear Mr. Larrier

Thank you for the promptness in sending over 'The Beast'. I really appreciate it. Sorry I did not call you last week but I was tied up with Estimates. I will, however, contact you earliest next week to set up a time when we can discuss the matter at hand.

Once again, I would like to thank you.

Yours sincerely

MIA AMOR MOTTLEY

# To fight the system first understand the nature of the 'Beast'.

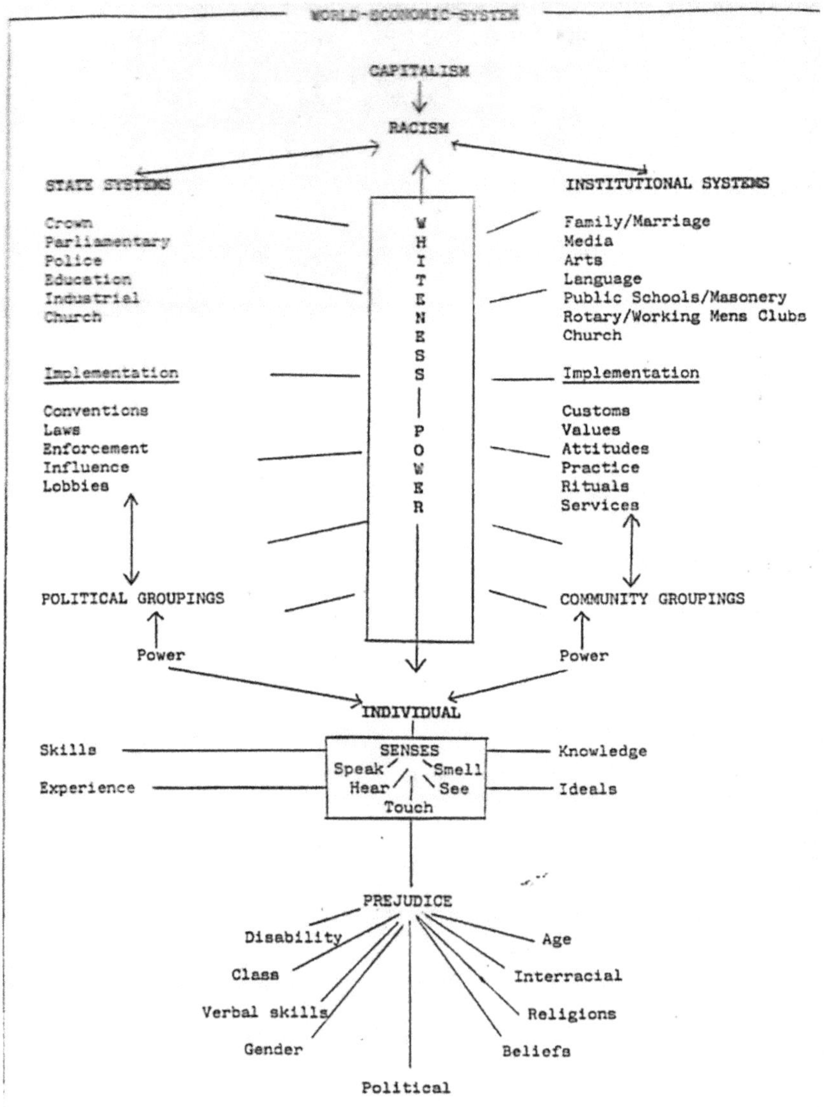

By 1998 it was clear to me that a change in African consciousness was imminent and I made public my view of what was to happen in the near future that would bring the changes needed to understand the system.



# Arthur's revolution

By Buddy Larrier

*"Ask not what your country can do for you, but what you can do for your country."*

THOSE words of wisdom from the late United States President John F. Kennedy reminded me that it is not often I hear anyone say my dream has come true, my mission is accomplished, or my vision has come to pass.

As I examine the Prime Minister's 1998 budget, I'm more convinced than ever that he is a visionary. The countdown towards the new millennium has started and the question of racism is seriously being addressed in the Caribbean.

Presently, there is an explosive situation developing in Guyana which needs serious action. Over the past three years, Prime Minister Owen Arthur and the Government of Barbados, in addressing the question of racism, have taken action best summarised as revolutionary.

For the first time, the history of Barbados has been put into proper perspective. Therefore, no self-respecting black persons should again present themselves as mouth-pieces for those who benefit from the evil of racism.

The government has established a Facilitation Unit for Returning Nationals, they have acknowledged Emancipation Day, August 1, as a National Holiday, and July 26 as a National Day of Significance, in remembrance of the social uprising of 1937.

Among the other significant initiatives taken are the introduction of African/Black Studies into the school curriculum; a National Heroes Day, April 28.

penal reform, lifting the stigma of "criminality" from those who had committed minor offences in former years; alternatives to prison and crime prevention as poverty is being addressed for the first time as a crime against humanity; public sector reform; constitutional reform, which is sure to end a fundamental aspect of the legacy of our colonial past, the removal of the Queen of England as Head of State of Barbados; and initiating the resurgence of a Federal Caribbean State.

These and many other initiatives taking place are all complementary factors to

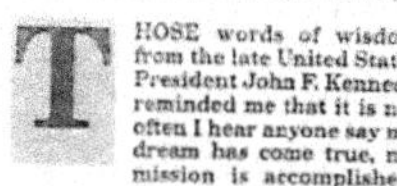


a vision I had of political awakening and consciousness, for the people of Barbados and the Caribbean generally, by the year 2000.

Until very recently, Barbados was regarded as racially backward; it was seen as the most conservative of all Caribbean countries. Some of the changes taking place are so fundamental that most Barbadians are unable to fully comprehend their significance.

It is acknowledged that the government has been able to take such revolutionary action because of the tremendous support from the progressive factions within society. The People's Forum, a combination of pressure groups such as the Pan-African Move-ment of Barbados, the Rastafari community, Ethiopian Orthodox Church, the African Nationalist Pioneer Movement (Clement Payne Movement — the Israel Lovell Foundation), and other consciously matured individuals who have been in the vanguard of lobbying for such changes.

## Great inspiration

On resettling in Barbados after 31 years of living abroad, I became associated with these progressive movements whose leaders have inspired me greatly as I sought to understand the dynamics of politics in Barbados. I'm particularly grateful to two gifted and dedicated Pan-Africanist comrades, Mr. David Comissiong and Trevor Prescod.

Mr. Comissiong, an attorney-at-law, a dynamic and conscientious "brother" who appears to be aware of his destiny and is therefore committed to the process of racial justice, is a political activist and parliamentary hopeful whose career in politics began with support for the Democratic Labour Party (DLP).

Comissiong subsequently joined the National Democratic Party (NDP), a group which broke away from the DLP in 1989. He had hoped that the NDP would have developed into a progressive force to implement programmes of action that would liberate the black

David Comissiong: "A conscientious brother who appears to be aware of his destiny".

populace. He has been disappointed with the unenlightened elements within that party.

Mr. Trevor Prescod is a historian, a conscientious person. His first political affiliation was with the BLP until, in his opinion, they were not progressive enough, and being influenced by a former comrade and government minister of that party, Mr. Don Blackman, he resigned and joined the DLP.

Soon afterwards, it became evident that the DLP was not fulfilling his desire to see genuine programmes which addressed the psychological problems of African Barbadians, and the difficulties of neo-colonialism. Prescod joined the NDP and along with Comissiong contested the 1994 elections as NDP candidates. As an independent candidate in that election, I also declared my intention to serve my country. Now both have agreed, like myself and other progressive Pan-Africanists, that the only way to ensure genuine empowerment under the leadership of the Right Hon. Owen Arthur, should be given maximum support. The Prime Minister is from the kind of background for which the BLP came into existence.

PM Owen Arthur: "In addressing the question of racism, (his government has) taken action best summarized as revolutionary."

Most conscious persons are of the opinion that the revolutionary policies of the government are no coincidence. We are convinced that Barbados is destined to make its mark on the world stage in a significant way.

It was a BLP government in the 1930s that first took up the mantle of political liberation for black Barbadians. It is the oldest political party in the English-speaking Caribbean. Out of the BLP in 1955, the DLP came into existence, and out of that party came the NDP. Over the years there has been a number of other parties and political organisations, but the DLP and NDP are the only two that have survived since the inception of the BLP in 1938.

Those of us who can analyse events of history would appreciate that we are at the most crucial period of world history. Therefore, the emergence of a reformed BLP Government to take the baton and lead Barbados and the Caribbean into the new millennium is understandable.

We are witnessing the resurgence of a spiritual dimension; the rebirth of our forefathers' spirit. Trevor Prescod has consented to rejoin the BLP, and will represent the party as its candidate in the general election constitutionally scheduled for September 1999. He will contest the seat for St. Michael's East constituency.

Trevor Prescod: "A conscientious person".

David Comissiong has accepted my invitation to spearhead the Barbados/OECS confederation initiative.

The government has also established an unprecedented Pan-Africanist Commission. The Commission's mandate is to further the interest of Barbadians in fostering better relationships and bonding with Africa and African descendants in the Diaspora.

The Commission will be under the directorship of David Comissiong, who has asked that I join him and Dr. Ikael Tafari to serve as members of the Commission's secretariat. This I consider to be a great honour and eagerly await to take up the position.

The highest honour of any citizen is to be selected to represent their country; therefore, to be asked to serve my country's interest at this level of taking a message of hope and liberation to our people is indeed a dream come true, a mission accomplished and should the government in its wisdom submit the draft resolution on Justice and Peace to the United Nations for October 12, to be designated a Universal Day of Hope, would be a vision come to pass.

The process of development and blessing for Barbados has come full circle. God's promises of blessing for Barbados are contained within the mandate of this commission. All Barbadians, black and white, at home and abroad, should be as excited as my colleagues and I of the opportunities open to us through this commission.

The commission will need the fullest cooperation and prayers if we are to succeed in this most difficult but exciting of tasks.

With the foundation firmly laid for a political revolution in African consciousness, on October 12, 2012 the government established a National Task Force on Reparations and I was invited to be a member of the committee. On October 12, 2013 I co-founded the Non-State Actors Reparations Commission Inc. as pursuant to the National Task Force, and the same year the World Social Forum proclaimed October 12 as the International Day for Reparations. On October 12, 2017 I had a meeting with Prime Minister Freundel Stuart, and shared aspect of my vision. I was seeking such a meeting with the Prime Minister of Barbados for over 40 years. However, the Prime Minister did not respond positively to the recommendations I made, therefore in May 2018 when the general election was called I decided to stand as an independent candidate for the same reasons I did in 1994 - to help bring about change, which I was confident would have taken place. Therefore, I told persons not to vote for me as I was not voting for myself. From my vision I do understand that we are in the time of fundamental changes. The political change of 2018 was unprecedented in Caribbean history.

My mission also includes bringing closure to my outstanding case against the British Health Authority for the violation of my human rights through the 1959 Mental Health Act. This act was introduced following the 1958 social disturbance in Nottingham and in London Notting Hill Gate. The act was part of the process of legally repatriating Caribbean nationals (British citizens) back to where they were born. The British Mental Health Act of 1959 was therefore part of the policies that has become known as the Windrush generation scandal. My case falls into that category and is believed by some to be unprecedented in British history.

Yet, today in the year 2021, the third decade of the 21st century, there are still persons who were born in the Caribbean but have lived in the United Kingdom from their childhood that are being deported back to the Caribbean, which is causing much distress for the families both in Britain and in the Caribbean. At present, one of the most topical discussions in the United Kingdom is that of the mental state and wellbeing within the black community - from emancipation to the Windrush generation scandal. This is most encouraging as it was four decades plus ago (1977) that I made my courageous stand against the abuse and human rights violations

# The Struggle For Justice Continues

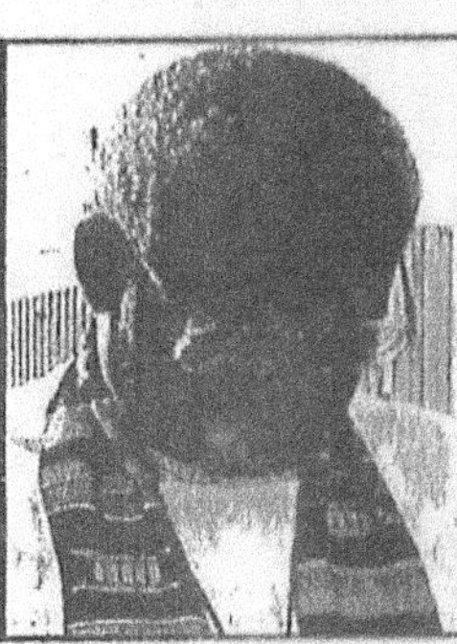



through the Mental Health Act of 1959. This act was revised but my pursuit for justice is ongoing.

In 2019, the Barbados Government initiated the We Gatherin' 2020 and Vision 2020 programme of targeting first, second and third generations Diaspora Barbadians to visit and to invest in Barbados. This Government's initiatives must have taken into consideration the work that was done by those of us who lived in the United kingdom from the 1950s and in particular the work done by, 'the Barbados Overseas & Friends Association' (BOFA), 'the Society for the Resettlement of Caribbean Nationals' (SRCN) and the Barbados Overseas Citizen Association (BOCA). The experiences of nationals who have lived outside of Barbados must be taken more seriously especially those who went to England in the 1950s and 1960s and are now referred to as Returning Nationals of the Windrush generation.

# The Delegation's Final Leg Of Country Visits Was Barbados

The Barbados Advocate, Monday, May 11, 1992

**THE ADVOCATE - MONDAY, MAY 11, 1992**

## Lifestyle

Can fish farming work here? *Page 20*

# Overseas group winds up fact-finding mission

*From left – Alfonso Jackman, Frank Jackman and Buddy Larrier: Barbadians who are living in England, but are determined to help the country deal with the present crises.*

*The four who were impressed with the mini parks being designed around the island elected to adopt the one in Gall Hill.*

On relocating to Barbados from England after some 30 plus years I was struggling to find a group of persons that I could relate to on the issues for which I was a leading activist in England. I was introduced to the Pan-African Movement that met each Wednesday at the Clement Payne Centre. It was from those meetings that I was motivated to join a religious group and was introduced to Archbishop Dudley Trotman who was seeking to establish a branch of a religious faith group in Barbados called the Anglican Rite Old Catholic Church that had its Headquarters in Texas USA. It was through this group that I was ordained. It was not long before it became clear to me that this faith group was not acceptable. I was then introduced to 'Universal Peace Federation' and took part in the Mongolian People' Federation for World Peace: World Assembly V in Seoul, South Korea in October 2006.

**MEMBERS OF ONE FAITH: (from left)** Father Rev. Dr. Valance Rudolph Humphrey, Rev. James Merlin Burgess, Rev. Sharon Diana Gittens, Rev. Aaron Larrier, Rev. Genoa Gertrude Dowdridge, Father Emerson Bellamy; background Archbishop Dudley Trotman and Bishop Wilmot John.

# Old Rite Catholics set up church in region

A NUMBER of recruits were recently ordained to the Anglican Rite Old Catholic Church.

The ordination of these new priests took place at the Headquaters of the Family Federation for World Peace, Long Bay, St. Philip. It was officiated by Archbishop Dr. Dudley Trotman, Bishop Wilmot John and Reverend Father Emerson Theodore Bellamy.

Those persons chosen to established the church in this region are Reverend James Merlin Burgess, Reverend Sharon Diana Gittens, Reverend Genoa Gertrude Dowdridge, Father Reverend Dr. Valance Rudolph Humphrey and Reverend Aaron Larrier.

The Old Catholic Church was founded in 1870 when it broke away from the Vatican and established the Old Catholic Movement outside The Netherlands.

The church has chapters in over 100 countries and Dr. Trotman is the Archbishop for the Caribbean. The headquarters are to be in Barbados.

However, I found that such groups were made up of persons that were articulating the struggles for unity and peace but did not want to call the Elephant in the room by its name. In England the word racism was on the lips of every conscious person. In Barbados this was not the case but the issues were the same. Therefore, I shortly left the Old Rite Catholics and join the African Methodist Episcopal (AME) Church, which has a very impressive history as the first civil society organisation in the western world that challenged racism in 1787; it was first called the Free African Society. However, I became disillusion in its leadership in Barbados and accepted that the time to move on had come.

In 2017 I had the opportunity of meeting the Honourable Minister Louis Farrakhan when he visited Barbados and after interacting with members from the Nation of Islam I began to see a change in some Barbadians as that organisation is ahead of most other groups. The teachings in the Nation of Islam encourage its members to call a spade a spade as the message in the book entitle 'Black Studies' attested.

This group home school their children and do not refer to them as KIDS, they also have an active programme of educating the community about addressing its needs through collective work. The group meets on Wednesdays to give the public an opportunity of finding out more about their aims and objectives. They do not seek to convert anyone to their way of life but share relevant information about the benefits of their faith towards living positively and for persons to know their history. However, on becoming more conscious of my African history I understood better my mission and am aware of the falsification of the images in the biblical story of Jesus Christ and the role that the Christian Church had played from the period of the Crusades through to the enslavement of African people and colonialism. Nevertheless, I am still holding strong to my faith in God the Creator, and I am now actively practising liberation theology as a founder member of the 'Ministry without walls' that was established in England in August 2019.

Along my journey there have been many persons that have encouraged and strengthened my 'Mission of Hope'. Once such person is the late legendary Professor Sydney Burnett-Alleyne.

This Barbadian who joined the ancestors on Tuesday, September 14, 2021 at age 93, lived in Exile in England from the 1980s of which the Barbados Government claims to be self-imposed while some claim otherwise. He was respected highly by many African leaders during their liberation struggle. This extra ordinary man was someone with whom I often has conversations and I was aware of his feelings towards Barbados, and of his desire before making the transition to visit the land of his birth. This he was willing and should have been allowed to do, if an appropriate question was raised on the floor of Parliament about his status, which should have been done during the We Gatherin' and or the vision 2020 programme.

Another person is the late Ben Ammi Ben-Israel founder and spiritual leader of the African Hebrew Israelites of Damona Israel (1939-2014).

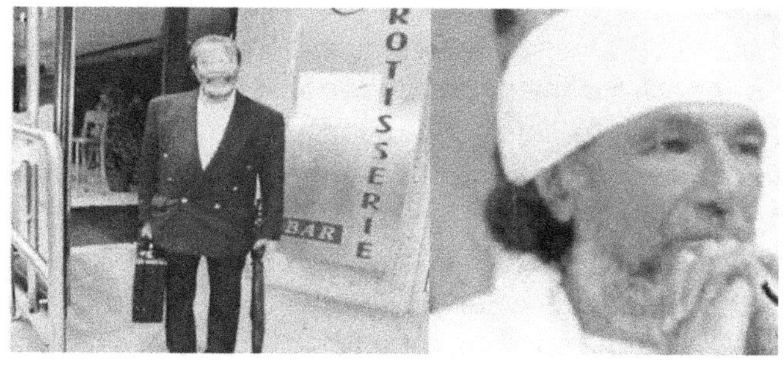

*(L) The late Professor Sydney Burnett-Alleyne*

*(R) The late Ben Ammi Ben-Israel*

Ben Ammi sent a delegation to both the 2001 United Nations World Conference against Racism held in Durban, South Africa and its follow-up the Afrikan and Afrikan Descendants World Conference against Racism held in Barbados in 2002. From the report he received of my mission and contribution at both conferences he invited me to Israel in December 2002 and 2003. To my surprised I was scrutinised by this spiritual Icon who was born on October 12, 1939. He then presented me with "The Broken Spear" – The New Jerusalem Peace Symbol that carry the words *"... and they shall beat their swords into plowshares, and their spears into pruning hooks; nations shall not lift up a sword against nation, neither shall they learn war anymore."* (Micah 4:3) I was charged with the responsibility of taking this symbol out of Israel for the first time. The African Hebrew Israelites of Jerusalem is working towards having a global conference in Barbados in August 2020.

Other spiritually committed persons that have help strengthened my

resolved to pursue my Mission of Hope are Deaconess Eloise Hintzen who was born in Guyana but has been living in England for many years and is the co-founder of our 'Ministry without walls', and Bishop Michael Steele a Diaspora Barbadian born in the United Kingdom, who is the founder of the international programme "The Class of Steele".

The most recent person that has convinced me of my destiny is His Excellency Benny Wenda, former chairman of the United Liberation Movement for West Papua, now designated president in waiting of an independent West Papua. I first met this warrior in the liberation struggle for his people in 2012 when he was on a visit to CARICOM countries seeking support for the independence of West Papua, which is presently under slave like occupation by Indonesia. Five years later in 2017 we met in Barbados again and it was through arranging a meeting for him with Prime Minister Freundel Stuart that I had the opportunity of officially meeting with the Prime Minister on October 12, 2017, which was after 40 years (1977 to 2017) of asking to have such a meeting with a Prime Minister of Barbados.

This was not the only challenge I faced. My claim for retroactive payment for work done from 1998 to 2001 was put to the three previous prime ministers. Also at one stage in 2016 while making my request I was informed by the parliamentary representative for the Christ Church South Constituency that the payment was approved, but I was not paid. This request was made throughout my tenure of two terms as one of the first cohorts of the Constituency Councils, which is prove to me that the liberation struggle for justice is continuous and that justice delayed is justice denied. In 2020 the struggle is being intensified. On Sunday, March 1 the Pan-Africanists in England joined the 21 days campaign against Racism started by the Pan-Africanists in Brazil which has been an annual event. In support of the event the Pan-Africanists in Canada has proclaimed March 2 as Black Mental Health Day.

# Champions In The Liberations Struggle Against Racism

## ▶PEOPLE

**BENNY WENDA,** (right) **leader of the West Papuan independence movement,** displaying his flag to Reverend Buddy Larrier, chairman of Decade For The People Of African Descent (Barbados Chapter).

(Picture by Rawle Culbard.)

# 'Help Papuans to become independent'

**THE WEST PAPUAN independence movement is appealing for outside help in securing their freedom from Indonesia.**

Benny Wenda, elected leader of the West Papuan movement, was recently in Barbados to galvanize support for their cause at the United Nations. That body has designated a decade for the people of African descent beginning next January 1, 2013.

"In the 1800s New Guinea was colonized by the British and the Dutch and divided up in two parts – West Papua and Papua New Guinea. In 1960 West Papua was promised independence from the Dutch who occupied my country.

"In 1963 before we were allowed full independence, my country was invaded by Indonesia," said Wenda.

He said that for the past 50 years Indonesia had silenced their cries for help.

"In our struggle for liberation an estimated 500 000 of our people have been murdered, killed and tortured," he said.

Benny said West Papuans were people of African descent who lived for years on their land before the Europeans invaded it in the 1800s.

"In 1969 at the United Nations General Assembly, a resolution was tabled to allow the people of West Papua to exercise their right to self-determination. The Government of Barbados was one of the signatories in support of the resolution.

"The resolution was defeated and my people are still under military occupation."

Wenda called on Barbados to join "other parliamentarians and other leaders across the world who are signing the West Papua Declaration in support of West Papua's freedom".

"As a leading country in this region for enlightenment, truth and justice, Barbados' support will give strength and encouragement to my people in their struggle against the Indonesian occupation". **(JS)**

"The main aim of The Gathering is to aid in the rebuilding of the nation. "Coming together in 2020 isn't about a single moment in time, but it is about a process.  It is about the building of a nation from St Lucy to St Philip, from the west coast to the east coast" under the theme Purposeful Pursuit of Barbadian Excellence", while reuniting Diaspora Barbadians (overseas nationals) with families at home and educating citizens and visitors alike of the importance of Barbados, parish by parish. Each parish is allocated a particular month and a theme for activities including family and community reunions. The programme was launched on January 1, in St. Lucy as the month of January is allocated to that parish with the theme faith. However, as the year has 12 months and Barbados only has 11 parishes, February is allocated for St. Peter – the theme in heritage, March is for St. Thomas - theme nature, April is for St. Joseph - theme adventure, May is for St. John - theme community, June is for St. George - theme Land, July is for St. Philip - theme

MARGARET COX LAYING flowers at the base of the commemorative plaque.

PRESIDENT of the Barbados National Union Of Fisherfolk Organisations Vernel Nicholls (left) Admiring the plaque bearing the names of 12 Fisherfolk who went missing at sea, two of whom were lost during the September 22, 1955 hurricane Janet. Looking on are fisheries offer Rolerick Sobers, secretary of the Christ Church South Constituency Council Stephanie Rice and council member Rev. Buddy Larrier whose father was one lost during Janet.

CAROL JONES accepting a trophy on behalf of her deceased father from fisheries officer Rolerick Sobers. (Pictures by Reco Moore)

sugar, August for St. Andrew - theme the Arts, September is for St. James - theme cricket, October for Christ Church - theme the Sea, November for St. Michael - food selling, and December is allocated to the City of Bridgetown for the whole Nation to come together with the theme friends and family. The parish of Christ Church is allocated the month of October with the theme the Sea. The Sea is very significant to the history of Barbados as it was by sea that we were colonized. The Sea has also claimed the lives of many of our people during the Atlantic crossing and of fishermen. Two plaques are mounted on the Berinda Cox Fish Market at Oistins in remembrance of fishermen who went missing at Sea and also of Hurricane Janet of September 22, 1955.

# BRIDGETOWN BARBADOS CITY OF PEACE

The first colony of England in the Caribbean (West Indies) was Barbados. It was colonized in 1627 with 80 Englishmen and 10 Africans. Barbados has the third oldest Parliament in the English-speaking world, after England and Bermuda. Barbados' capital city of Bridgetown and its Garrison is a UNESCO World Heritage Site.

The 10 Africans that arrived with the English were captured from a Portuguese ship by the English en route to Barbados. African enslavement from the continent, West Africa in particular, did not start until the 1640s. Between 1627 and the 1640s white Europeans mainly from Ireland and Scotland and some poor English made up the slave labour as indentured servants. It is believed that the majority of Africans brought to Barbados included the Asante, Ewe, Fon and Fante peoples that provided the bulk of imports into Barbados. Nigeria also provided captives for enslavement in Barbados, these were mainly Yoruba, Efik, Igbo and Ibibio being the main ethnic groups targeted. Barbados became the first and only total slave society.

Barbados has a long history of slave rebellions. During the 1600's, there were three unsuccessful rebellions in 1649, 1675 and 1692. The rebellion of 1692 was also island-wide with over 200 enslaved persons arrested and over 90 executed after being found guilty of rebellion. The 1692 rebellion so traumatized the enslaved that it took 124 years until 1816 before there was another rebellion in Barbados, which was due to an increase in free blacks and enslaved persons born on the island. During the 1816 rebellion known as the Bussa rebellion more than 800 enslaved persons were killed while fighting and over 100 executed after the war. This was the first rebellion of this size in Barbados and the Caribbean and took part for three (3) days on the southern part of the island. This rebellion caused reform to ease the hardships of slavery. It is therefore understandable why Benny Wenda of the United Liberation Movement of West Papua was spiritually drawn to Barbados to help with the slave like situation in West Papua under Indonesia military occupation. Truth, Justice and Peace is the order for 2021 and beyond. In 2014 a progressive NGO made an application to the International Cities of Peace Organisation for Heritage Bridgetown Barbados to be listed as a City of Peace. Taking into consideration the unprecedented murders that took place in Barbados in 2019 and with the government action of We Gatherin' 2020 and Vision 2020 programme a concerted effort by some business persons is building on the 2014 initiative by the NGO to have the capital city of Bridgetown become a vibrant City of Peace that would complement what the government is presently doing to transform the city. There was to be a Welcome Centre for persons visiting Barbados and wanting information on the history of the city and for Diaspora Barbadians seeking information on how to make their transition in resettling easy. The Welcome Centre was to be located at Mall 34, Broad Street until COVID-19 hit Barbados. Efforts were also being made for an Epic Centre located at the Jackie Opel Amphitheatre at the General Post Office for culture activities including weekly lecture on Barbados' history, unity and peace through a programme of lobbying for a resolution to be presented to the United Nations for October 12 as the International Day for Reparations for truth, justice, peace, healing and reconciliation. It is our desire for Barbados to be recognized globally as the first nation state of peace.

## Recommendation

The reason for the proposal of October 12 to be designated as the International Day for Reparations for Truth, Justice, Peace, Healing, and Reconciliation is because history has informed us that the date October 12, 1492 was when Columbus' expedition made landfall in the Caribbean. The legacy resulting from that historic event has impacted on the lives of every known person living in the world today. The impact has been mostly negative on black people of African descent and on indigenous people of the Americas and the Caribbean. We are of the view that the unprecedented events taking place around the world points to the fact that change is at hand and that CARICOM is playing a leading role in the change.

The African state of Ghana commemorated the 400th anniversary of African enslavement by Britain in the United States of America 1619 to 2019 with the 'Year of Return'. The We Gatherin' 2020 by Barbados is building on that initiative by Ghana to reunite Diaspora Barbadians (overseas nationals) with families at home through activities relevant to each parish with each parish being allocated a particular month and a theme, which is very timely, and the Vision 2020 programme is preparing for the 400th anniversary of Barbados as a colony governed by Britain from 1627 to 2027. The UDOHT is of the view that the proposal mentioned above should be supported as we are approaching the 400th anniversary of Barbados. A new Barbados will ensure the economic and spiritual liberation of African people. It was through the Barbados slave Code Act of 1661 that the black man/woman was denigrated to the status of chattel less than human. Therefore, my spirit compels me to believe that it is incumbent upon Barbados, now as Chair of CARICOM Reparations Commission sub-committee for reparations with the first female Prime Minister, to be asked to table the resolution to the United Nations on behalf of CARICOM that now has a seat on the security council of the United Nations by way of Saint Vincent and the Grenadines.

The NGO that has been making recommendations to world leaders is also lobbying the Heads of CARICOM on three matters of great importance. We are asking for the support of civil society NGOs and media houses across the region to assist us in our endeavours. The matters are:-

**(1)    that CARICOM table a resolution to the United Nations that October 12 be designated as the International Day for Reparations;**

**(2)    that the capital city of each CARICOM country be proclaimed a City of Peace towards the Caribbean becoming a practical Zone of Peace and;**

**(3)    that a Reparations Lottery Fund be established in each CARICOM country to educate nationals**

**about reparations and in the process help in lifting black people out of generational poverty.**

In addition, our idea to assist in moving Barbados forward is that during We Gatherin' the people of St. Philip should proclaim the month of **July as Family Unity Month** and the people of Christ Church proclaim **October as Justice and Peace Month**. If these were done, they might help reduce the senseless murders if not bringing them to an end because children from their primary school will be taught of the importance of family unity and peace. We will then be able to introduce a programme to the children of Sports for Peace to cultivate a Culture of Peace in Barbados and by extension the Caribbean.

The conscious movements for unity and for peace have been taken to other levels and the Barbados Government and CARICOM should take note. On Saturday, February 22 over 1300 youth from the Boys Scout and the Girls Guides were on the streets of Bridgetown marching for unity and on Sunday, February 23 some 60 Bishops from 19 countries gathered to hear the words from Pope Francis who addressed a conference in Spain entitled the 'Mediterranean Frontier of Peace'. Peace and unity are the foundation of the right to Self-Determination and Reparations in the Caribbean region. Therefore, the call from the people of Bonaire, Saint Eustatius (Statia) Saba, Curaçao, Saint Maarten and Aruba and other nations that are still under colonial government must be heard by CARICOM who needs to consider more seriously the right to Self-Determination and Reparations because the Caribbean is in a post-colonial war, and need to give due recognition to the issue of the self-determination of the remaining non-independent Caribbean countries in the region as unfinished business. This could be done by having Self-Determination and decolonization placed on the permanent agenda of the CARICOM Heads of Government meetings. The organization, Nos Kier Boneiru Bek ( We Want Bonaire Back) in Partnership with Caribbean Progressive Alliance are planning to go with a group to New York representing eleven Caribbean dependencies / islands NGO's and to organize a Colloquium in New York close to the United Nations Headquarters entitle **"Self-Determination and Reparations - The Future of**

**the Non-Independent Caribbean and South America"** from March 20th to 28th as this coincides and in conjunction with the 25th March, 2020 Commemoration of the International Day of Remembrance of the Victims of Slavery and the Transatlantic Slave Trade at the United Nations (U.N.) Headquarters in New York where U.N. Secretary-General, Mr António Guterres and representatives of U.N. Member States are expected to speak. The main objective for this colloquium is to raise awareness of the international community and the United Nations of the urgent, unfinished process of decolonization in the Caribbean and South American region. CARICOM should be represented at this meeting to give support to the liberation efforts of our people. At its 31st intersession Heads of Government meeting held in Barbados a consensus was reached on the matter of violence and crime that they are not only law and justice issues but that they are also health related issues, which means psychological health issues.

The information shared in this booklet should encourage persons who read it to get a copy of my other books soon to be published that includes; 'The Beast the Devil's Friend' that gives insights into why the coronavirus is among us at this time; 'Against the Edge – Patient or Prisoner', which would give insights as to why the policies now known as the Windrush generation scandal is having such an impact on CARICOM states with persons being repatriated from the United Kingdom; 'Pride and Unity - The Dawn of a New Era', and 'From Africa to Barbados and back', which would shed some light on why it has taken a female prime minister of Barbados to make the necessary historic links between Barbados in Africa. These books are all part of my mission resulting from my vision of 1977.

The present world problem with ethnic racial groups was started with the Barbados Slave Code Act of 1661. This is the year 2021 and Barbados has launched a vision 2020 programme, which means that Barbadians should now have perfect eye sight, perfect hearing and understanding to correct what was started in 1661. The invitation for Diaspora Barbadians to return home and to invest their knowledge has been an ongoing process for many years in particular from Barbadians who lived in the United Kingdom. This was evident by the seven associations for returning nationals that were formed from 1994 as all were by persons who had resettled from England. It was the initiative of these persons that encouraged the government in 1996 to establish the Facilitating Unit for Returning Nationals (FURN) under the leadership of Mr. Jeffrey Hunte. FURN later became known as the Barbados Network and is now the We Gatherin' programme. The photo is of the founding members of the Umbrella Organisation for Returning Nationals that was directed to be established by Prime Minister Owen Arthur:- Reuben Rollock, Richard Cutting, Dorrett Foster, Wilbert Haynes, Pam Clarke, Buddy Larrier, Verita Williams, Juliette Bryan, Hazel Roissetter, Errol Hunte, Edgar Lynch, Douglas Griffith and others.

There are other persons who had demonstrated their willingness to invest in Barbados to whom I am personally indebted, these include the following persons who supported my endeavours over the years; Pauline Lashley, Hoebert Payne, Sybil & Joseph Phoenix, Lewis Boyce, Sheila Springer, Adolphus Grazette, Elsie Foster, Henderson Kirton, Nyle Hall, James Bryan, Esther Daniel, Kathleen Leacock – Myrie, Clinton Lyder, Doris Skeete, David Corbin, Darcey Clarke and Dennis Sargent among others.

The named persons above do not all have Barbadian roots but they all wanted to make contributions to the development of Barbados and to CARICOM but was uncertain how best to do so. I convinced some of them to join a collective and to invest in a pilot project which they did. Some of these same persons are now looking at the opportunities that We Gatherin' and Vision 2020 may have to offer. It is my hope that they will seize opportunities now available through the initiatives of CARICOM and in particular that Guyana presents with its large oil and gas discoveries. This will be the second time that the doors of Guyana have been open to people of the Caribbean. In the 1960 Linden Forbes Sampson Burnham had invited Caribbean people to come to Guyana and help develop the country instead of going to England. Today people of African descent in particular our youth of Caribbean families in the Diaspora, which has been designated as the Sixth Region of Africa must look to CARICOM and to Africa for their salvation. The countries of CARICOM should use the We Gatherin' by Barbados and the Saint Lucia Diaspora Affairs Unit as examples to target our youths. This has been part of my mission from 1977.

To the persons mentioned above I say thank you for helping me to keep hope alive.

## Books Pending

- 'The Beast The Devil's Friend' (Revised)

- 'Against The Edge – Patient Or Prisoner' (Revised)

- 'From Africa To Barbados And Back'

- 'Historic Oistins And Its Fishing Community'

*The vision was "a vivid picture of a New Political and Economic Order for the 21st century based on truth, justice, peace, healing, and reconciliation; new political awakening for Barbadian and other people of the Caribbean region, as leaders in world affairs; the uniting of his family as a single unit towards unity of African people; the acquisition of economic power by black people and the end of Apartheid in South Africa and of global oppression of 'White Supremacy' (Racism)".*

*Given in May 1977, made public 1989*

## This vision demands that the Caribbean be A Zone of Peace

My opinion is that God has ordained that Bridgetown be the first City of Peace in CARICOM towards the Caribbean becoming a practical Zone of Peace, one city at a time; that October 12 be the International Day for Reparations towards truth, justice, peace, healing and reconciliation; that July be the African Family Unity Month inclusive of a Family Unity Day. To confirm that these are spiritual the following are indicators. My grandmother, mother, father and I, a daughter and two grand children were all born under the star sign of Cancer in July. My eldest daughter's only child was to be born on July 2 - the same birth date as my grandmother, mother and I, but I strongly objected because her father was not a black man, so my daughter had her delivered by cesarean section on

July 1, 1993. I paid a heavy price for letting my prejudices interfered with God's plan. Then to my astonishment came the birth of my eldest son's first child, a daughter from a German woman in 1995. She was two years old before I found out that her date of birth was October 12. These events cannot be written off as coincidences; no, they represent a mighty God with plans.

## A CHANGING WORLD

To fully appreciate the importance of the messages in this small booklet I shall summarised the text by asking you to seriously consider the vision I received in May 1977, drawing to your attention some events that took place in 2021 (1) Pope Francis proclaimed July 30 as the International Day for the elderly and grandparents (2) the United Nations designated August 31 as the International Day for People of Afrikan Descent and (3) the historic occasion of September 7 when leaders of the African Union and CARICOM held a virtual summit to discuss plans of working closer together for the unity of the global Afrikan family and (4) the 76th session of the United Nations General Assembly that was held from Monday, September 21st with the theme; "Building Resilience Through Hope" included a special session on September 22nd of a historic occasion on the matter of Reparations for Afrikan people.

The events mentioned above contextualise my vision and works over the past 40 plus years. In addition the COVID-19 pandemic that is impacting the minds of people worldwide is similar to what I experienced back in 1977 when I visualized a new world order for the 21st Century. Some of the messages contain in this booklet include my message to the people of the world for the second time; the first occasion was in 1990 after I became aware of a programme to depopulate the world by two billion people. Since 1990 I have learned much of world affairs. I note with great interest that on Tuesday, September 22 while addressing the general assembly of the UN the Prime Minister of Great Britain the Hon. Boris Johnson made a speech on the matter of climate change in which he referred to the history of humankind. This was most revealing to me as it was the first time I have heard a Caucasian person speak to the matter of modernity in such a manner. He informed us that from modernity to this present year 2021 of the 21st Century there has never been a more confusing and challenging period. I felt obliged to present this message in three parts: modernity, the 15th to 20th Century and the 21st Century, which covers three periods; the Doctrine of Discovery, the Barbados Slave Code and the Manifest Destiny all leading to the present situation in the world.

## Modernity

To participate in modernity was to conceive of one's society as engaging in organizational and knowledge advances that makes one's immediate predecessors appear antiquated or, at least, surpassed. If we adequately reflect on history from the 15th Century to the present we should come to the conclusion that the changes now taking place due to the Black Lives Movement and the pandemic is necessary. The Caucasian ethnic group have had a long history of perpetuating brutality on its people; example such as burning at the stake, feeding people to the lions and gladiators competition to mention a few, these were done as entertainment for people.

## The 15th Century; Doctrine of Discovery

From the late 15th Century there has been an on-going war between Caucasians and Afrikans – or non-white people. There is much evidence that the war is not only about flesh and blood but also against powers and principalities of wickedness in high places. For many years Afrikans with high melanin content (black people) were treated by Caucasians (white people) as if we had a virus; measures of Apartheid, lynching, segregation and social distancing were imposed. Today similar measures are being imposed by white people on some white people and on most black people.

It is therefore necessary that we examine and understand why there is this need for a radical change. From January 1492 the world has been undergoing change due to wars of various political and religious governances seeking control over the people of the world under the pretext of doing God's works. A peculiar war started when the Black Moors that were ruling Spain for hundreds of years were defeated by the White Christians at the battle of Grenada. That victory ushered in a process of world transformation similar to what is still on-going. In August of 1492 Christopher Columbus was sent on an exploratory mission with three small ships: the Niña, the Pinta and the Santa Maria. The expedition made landfall in Ayiti (Haiti) the Caribbean (West Indies) on October 12, 1492. He returned to Spain in December that year with two ships as the Santa Maria was shipwrecked. On reporting what he had found to those who had sent him on the mission, and of the kindness and friendly nature of the people he had encountered to which he provide evidence of their kindness and the assistance they offered and a home they provided for members of his crew that were left behind due to the loss of Santa Maria. Months later in September 1493 Columbus was sent back to the Caribbean region on a different mission. This time with 17 war ships and 1200 mercenaries that were recruited from the prisons, and with written instructions from Pope Alexander V1 namely the **"Doctrine of Discovery"**, a detailed action plan of how the indigenous people were to be governed and why all the lands of any people that were not Christians were to be confiscated and bequeath to a European Crown and rule by Christians; and that all such peoples were to be Christianised or enslaved, and if they resisted that they be killed. At the time there was not a common agreement among Caucasians to accept the term Christian; most Europeans could not graph the spiritual dimension of the term Christian. Those periods included three major inquisitions; the Spanish, Portuguese and Roman all seeking to dominate their known world.

The Doctrine of Discovery was initially enforced throughout the Americas and the Caribbean; the grabbing of other peoples' lands was soon extended to all continents. Colonialism spread as if it was a pandemic, a virus of white supremacy (racism).

## The 17th Century; Barbados Slave Code

After 154 years of grabbing other peoples' land the small island of Barbados was colonized by England in 1627 and subsequently became the flagship of the British Empire for promoting slavery. There was an unusual occurrence when it was colonized as there were no people on the island. Its development therefore started with 80 English men and 10 Afrikans that was captured from a Portuguese ship en route to Barbados. The island soon became the first and only total slave society. It was the place where the practice of breaking a man/woman and making a slave was perfected. After the execution of King Charles 1 in 1649 in 1651 following there was a battle between the Republic of England and its colony Barbados, which resulted in the 1652 Barbados Peace Charter. By 1661 England had regain royal status after Charles 11 was crown King of England. By then the process of enslavement was so well established that the governing elite enacted the Barbados Slave Code stating in law that black people were not full human being. This was the first such law to speak of an ethnic group of the human family as chattels - things to be owned by others. This could be considered as a new variant of the deadly disease call racism. The island became a trans-shipment point of enslaved people for Great Britain, which soon became the dominant slave Empire.

## The 19th Century; Manifest Destiny

To promote the British Empire the Barbados Slave Code was enforced in other Caribbean countries before being adopted in the USA and becoming part of its constitution in which it was stated that black people were only 3/5 human being. This idea was brought about because George Washington had visited Barbados in 1751 where he learned of the Slave Code. By 1845 the USA constitution had become popular, and the American legislators then introduced a doctrine call the **'Manifest Destiny'** with an ideology and the idea that the USA was destined by God to expand its dominance and spread democracy and capitalism across the entire North American continent. This resulted in all colonializing nations adopting the concept of black inferiority as a practice for their governance, which brought about the concept of a white collective ethnic group/race. Their action motivate the enslaved Afrikans to intensify the process of collective liberation, which was most evident in the case of the attempted slave rebellion in Barbados in 1675 to overthrow the white elite and established an Afrikan Kingdom. This was followed with the successful revolution of enslaved Afrikans of Haiti that took on European nations in a revolution that started on August 31, 1791 and ended on January 1, 1804 when Haiti became the first free independent nation state; declaring that any enslaved Afrikan that reached Haiti would be a free Afrikan. The Haiti revolution advanced the emancipation process with the passing of the slave trade acts in 1807 and 1808 and the Emaciation Act of 1834 that took effect in the British colonies in 1838. It then became necessary for the white group to put aside some of their differences and to act with one accord. This was done fifty years after the British Empire emancipated its enslaved people. The 1884-5 Berlin conference was held for European nations to take control of the continent of Afrika; to carve it up and share the spoils (countries) among themselves as they did the Americas and Caribbean.

## The 20th Century; European collaboration

This uneasy unity between European nations had some challenges and between 1914 and 1918 there was a family dispute (First World War) and again between 1939 and 1945 (Second World War) following which the League of Nations (present day United Nations) was established. In 1990 as Europeans were preparing to commemorate the 500th anniversary (1992) of Columbus arrival in the Caribbean a plan was put in place to bring about greater unity between them; an initiative known as the European Union (EU) was put in place in preparation for the 21st Century. It is well known that the lands of black people have all kinds of minerals that are essential for the continuation of world development. If the goal of Caucasians from the 15th Century were to seize the lands of black people for economic fortunes then in this 21st Century with high information technology the lands without many black people become attractive and necessary for Caucasians maintenance of world dominance. The problem with that idea is that Afrikan black people have awakened and we are reclaiming our lands and our cultural inheritances that were stolen, and we are seeking reparatory justice. It is therefore reasonable to understand why the Caucasians would feel that they have no option other than to depopulate the world of mainly black people.

In 1900 the first conference of Afrikans from the continent and from its Diaspora was held in London. Pursuant to this were the Universal Negro Improvement Association and Afrikan Communities League (UNIA) holding the first International Convention of the Negro Peoples of the World in August of 1920, where the Honourable Marcus Mosiah Garvey presided as Chairman, and at which time he was elected Provisional President of Afrika. A document was created during that first international convention held from the first to the thirty-first of the month of August, called the "Declaration of Rights of the Negro Peoples of the World." It contains 12 complaints and 54 articles drafted and adopted at the convention by the thousands of representatives of the 400 million Afrikan people in the Diaspora. It was proclaimed "that the 31st day of August of each year to be an International holiday to be observed by all Negroes."

## Unusual Events Influencing World History

The Marcus Garvey life story is still influencing Afrikan people today. Pursuant to the 1920 event in New York an unusual event happened in Barbados the consequences of which is now impacting on the world; there was a birth of a child on July 2, 1943 that coincidentally shares the same birth date as both his mother and grandmother; what is even more unusual is that there is another family in New Mexico with the same experience and circumstances as the Barbados family, sharing the same birth date.

In 1955 Barbados experienced a most devastating hurricane, which claimed the life of some 38 people including the father of the child that was born on July 2, he was a fisherman and went missing at sea during the hurricane. As a result the family benefited more than most from Hurricane Janet. In 1977 while living in England the July 2 birth day man had an epiphany with a vision for the 21st Century, which he could not put into words until 1989 after visiting Afrika for the first time.

## Scriptures Reference To Life Experiences

Sometimes a passage of scripture can explain a person's life experience, as in the book of Jeremiah 1: 4-9 (Before I formed thee in the belly I knew thee – and I ordained thee a prophet unto the nations). Pursuant to his Afrikan visit he then became aware of a plan to depopulate the world by two billion of mainly black people. His vision has five aspects; (1) *"a New Political and Economic World Order for the 21st century base on truth and justice;* (2) *New political awakening for Barbadians and other people of the Caribbean region (Diaspora);* (3) *the uniting of his family as a single unit as a sign of hope towards the unity of African people (Barbados is renowned for family reunions started by his family in 1978);* (4) *the acquisition of economic power of 'black people (reparations);* (5) *the end of Apartheid in South Africa and of Global oppression of 'White Supremacy (Racism)"* (the present consciousness taking place worldwide).

While sharing the vision he was compulsory sectioned into a mental institution. Resulting from his detention he coincidentally created history in England with reference to the 1959 Mental Health Act. The quote above is taken from his first book in 1989 entitled; "Pride & Unity the Dawn of a New Era – Barbados and the Larrier family Unit".

## Conclusion

There are two dates that should be of particular interest to Afrikan people in the liberation process, October 12 and August 31. It was on October 12, 1492 that there was a clash of cultures to start a new world transformation when Christopher Columbus arrived in the Americas / Caribbean, which resulted in the greatest war the world has ever known; against indigenous people and enslaved people of the new world. Haiti started its revolutionary battle of the war on August 31, 1791; In 1920 Marcus Garvey highlighted the importance of August 31, and called for it to be an international day for Negro people of the world. In 2001 the United Nations brought the people of the world together for the greatest world conference the world has known on August 31 to discuss racism; the most complex subject matter resulting from October 12, 1492.

This booklet is therefore a clarion call for both the 'Doctrine of Discovery' and the Barbados Slave Code Act of 1661 in particular, to be repealed, which will bring about an end to the ideology of white supremacy (Racism), which is necessary if people of the world are to experience the love of God. The present worldwide coronavirus pandemic has created the perfect atmosphere and setting for a mental health pandemic that is necessary for the minds of all the people to be transformed. Black people in particular have a chance to stand up to the colonial dictates and reclaim our minds from that of a slave mentality. Such is the instructions given by many of our esteem revolutionary ancestors including His Imperial Majesty Haile Selassie 1 and His Excellency Marcus Masiah Garvey. Freeing our minds from mental slavery would be advanced speedily if the governments of Barbados and CARICOM would support the proclamation by the World Social Forum that October 12 be the International Day for Reparations that would promote truth, justice, peace, healing and reconciliation for the people of the world. For hundreds of years the date October 12 was proclaimed by Caucasians as both 'Columbus Day' and 'Discovery Day' and during that period many untruths about black people were told and accepted within all ethnic and cultural groups. In recent times the date October 12 has been claimed by Indigenous Peoples for them to tell the world of their history and to reclaim their lands, which command the attention that reparatory justice is necessary and is due. The world is now in a crisis as never before and is crying out for change. Afrika and its worldwide Diaspora is coming closer and Afrikans need to find solutions to Afrika's problem.

## The Solution

Part of the solution is the pursuit of truth and justice and for truth to be spoken to power. Barbados is advancing towards becoming a parliamentary republic by November 30, and will seek to leave its colonial pass behind. Because of its peculiar history the eyes of the world is on Barbados; therefore, there could not be a more opportune time than now for the resolution about October 12 to be tabled to the United Nations. It has been before the government of Barbados from as far back as May 1995. The same draft resolution was presented to the UN World Conference in 2001 at Durban, South Afrika and was also endorsed at the first follow-up to Durban, the Afrikan and Afrikan descendants' world conference against racism held in Barbados in October 2002. Acknowledging the fact that the date October 12 has impacted on all the worlds' peoples in 2012 Barbados established a National Taskforce on Reparations, pursuant to which in 2013 the World Social Forum adopted the principle of the draft resolution and proclaimed October 12 as the International Day for Reparations. In 2015 Mr. David Comissiong (now H.E. David Comissiong) while representing the Barbados Reparations Taskforce made a recommendation to a gathering of CARICOM nationals which was held in Antigua and Barbuda, asking their support for October 12 as an International Day for Reparations. His recommendation must have influenced CARICOM Reparations Commission that have also adopted the principle of the draft resolution; and in 2017 proclaimed October 12 as Caribbean Holocaust Day. All that is required now is for the government of Barbados to table the resolution to the UN on behalf of CARICOM. It can't be coincidental that between June and July 2021 Barbadians experience 46 thousands strikes of lightning in less than two minutes and its second hurricane in 66 years and that it happened on the date of that strange birth date July 2 of two families.

On September 7 the African Union and CARICOM held a historic virtual summit under the theme; "Unity across Continents and Oceans: Opportunities for Deepening Integration". Let the creator God and our ancestors be our guide and let all Afikan led organizations call on the Governments of CARICOM and the African Union to ensure that the resolution for October 12 is tabled to the UN in 2021.

The historic event of Barbados the first Small Island State to have hosted the UN Trade and Development conference from Monday, October 3 to Thursday, October 7 just two weeks after the 76th session of the UN with the theme; Building Resilience Through Hope is an indication that the world is paying attention to the messages that Barbados is sending for there to be a better world order base upon truth, justice, peace, healing and reconciliation with LOVE for all of God's creation.

It is therefore necessary for the matter of THEM vs. US that was made lawful that a section of the human family could be treated as less than human – as chattel, a thing to be owned by others, which was started with the Barbados Slave Code of 1661 be brought to an end. In 2001 the first world conference of the 21st Century the United Nations World Conference against Racism, Racial Discrimination, Xenophobia and Related intolerance reached a consensus that seek to correct that dehumanising slave code act of 1661. The conference concluded with the Declaration and Programme of Action stating that the transatlantic trade in Afrikans, chattel enslavement and colonialism were all crimes against humanity and that Reparations is rightly due to the descendants of enslaved people and for the evils of colonialism to be exposed and corrected. In 2021 the UN at its 76th session from Monday September 21 with the theme "Building Resilience through Hope" held a special session on Reparations on Tuesday 22. This was the first such session on reparatory justice for people of Afrikan ancestry. This historic occasion was followed by the 15th session of the UN trade and development, which was held in Barbados; making Barbados the first small island state to have hosted the event.

These historic events are relevant to the initiative that was taken in 2019 by Her Excellency Ambassador Arikana Chihombori Quao MD - Founder and President of the African Diaspora Development Institute (ADDI), which is the latest Pan-Afrikanists' endeavour seeking to bring all the various organisations into one accord; with one aim and one destiny of making the continent of Afrika what we want it to be for the betterment of all Afrikan people. I am honoured to have been asked to establish the Barbados chapter of ADDI, which is not coincidental to have been registered during the week of the 15th UN session of trade and development and when the President of Kenya Uhuru Muigai Kenyatta was given the highest honour of Barbados - the Freedom of Barbados for his contribution towards uniting the two regions Afrika and its Diaspora. The Barbados chapter of ADDI was launched during a live stream event on October 12, 2021. We give thanks and praises to God the creator and to our ancestors. The future looks much brighter now than it did yester year.